D0791833

"Blues to me is life. Life the way we live it, life the way we lived in the past and the way, I believe, we will live it in the future. It has to do with people, places, and things, and that's why it is here to stay."

—B. B. KING

THE BLUES: BIRTH OF AN AMERICAN SOUND

By Pamela Dell

Content Adviser: Christine M. Kreiser,
Blues Revue *magazine*

The Child's World

Published in the United States of America by The Child's World®
PO Box 326
Chanhassen, MN 55317-0326
800-599-READ
www.childsworld.com

The Child's World®: Mary Berendes, Publishing Director
Editorial Directions, Inc.: E. Russell Primm, Editorial Director; Emily J. Dolbear,
Line Editor; Katie Marsico, Assistant Editor; Matthew Messbarger, Editorial Assistant;
Susan Hindman, Copy Editor; Sarah E. De Capua, Proofreader; Marsha Bonnoit,
Peter Garnham, Terry Johnson, Chris Simms, and Stephan Carl Wender,
Fact Checkers; Tim Griffin/IndexServ, Indexer; Dawn Friedman,
Photo Researcher; Linda S. Koutris, Photo Selector

Cover photograph: New Orleans blues legend Lizzie Miles / © Bradley Smith/Corbis

Interior photographs ©: Bradley Smith/Corbis: 2; Bettmann/Corbis: 8, 9, 15, 20, 24, 25, 30, 34;
Marion Post Wolcott/Corbis: 16; Terry Cryer/Corbis: 31; Tim Mosenfelder/Corbis: 35; Craig Lovell/
Corbis: 36; MPI/Getty Images: 6, 11; Hulton Archive|Getty Images: 21, 22; Frank Driggs Collection/
Getty Images: 26, 28, 29, 32; Mike Moore/Getty Images: 33; The Granger Collection, New York: 23;
Marion Post Wolcott, Farm Security Administration-Office of War Information Collection/
Library of Congress: 12; Alan Lomax/Library of Congress: 14, 17, 18.

Library of Congress Cataloging-in-Publication Data
Dell, Pamela.
The blues : birth of an American sound / by Pamela Dell.
p. cm. — (Journey to freedom)
Includes bibliographical references and index.
ISBN 1-59296-230-0 (library bound : alk. paper)
1. Blues (Music)—History and criticism—Juvenile literature. I. Title. II. Series.
ML3521.D45 2004
781.643—dc22   2004000244

Contents

IN THE 1850s, COTTON PICKERS WORK THE FIELDS NEXT TO AN OVERSEER ON HORSE-BACK. ENSLAVED WORKERS OFTEN SANG IN THE FIELDS. BLUES MUSIC PROBABLY HAS ITS ROOTS IN THE FIELD HOLLER.

Roots of the Blues

I would rather be dead and six feet in my grave,
I would rather be dead and six feet in my grave,
Than to be way up here, honey, treated this a-way.
—From "Cypress Grove Blues"
by Skip James (1931)

Several hundred years ago, enslaved Africans began toiling on the plantations of the American South. Their children, born in the United States, were enslaved, too. For many generations, they lived as the wrongful property of others. Most slaves were forced to work in the fields growing tobacco, cotton, and other crops. They worked from before sunrise until late in the day. They worked in the bitter cold and in the blistering heat. They usually worked all year long, with barely a day off.

Most of the time, the enslaved people were forbidden even from speaking as they worked. But the workers found ways to express their feelings of hopelessness. Often a worker in the fields might raise his or her voice and cry out a few words with a shred of mournful melody. Hearing such cries, other enslaved workers would answer in a similar way, repeating the words they had heard or adding a new line. Like this, a song would take shape.

This natural expression of intense feeling became known as a field holler. The field holler helped lift the spirits of the workers and pass the time more quickly. It was often a response to the burden of a life lived without freedom, usually until death. It also provided a link to lost African customs that the slaves were no longer allowed to practice. Many historians think that these call-and-response songs, so full of sorrow, were probably where the music known as the **blues** began.

"The blues" as an expression has been around since at least 1807, when the words appeared in the work of American writer Washington Irving. Even in the 1600s, Europeans called sad or depressed feelings the "blue devils." Blues **lyrics** have always dealt with these troubled states of mind.

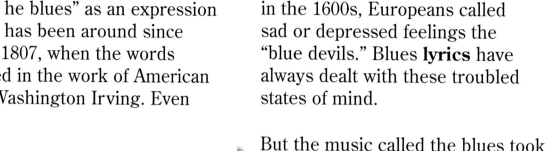

But the music called the blues took form gradually. Throughout the South, enslaved workers were forced to drop their African religions and take up Christianity. The call-and-response songs began to blend with church hymns. The result was deeply felt songs with religious or biblical themes known as spirituals. Their lyrics spoke of being carried out of slavery, of being lifted up by the Lord's grace, and of reaching the Promised Land. All these themes gave hope to the thousands of enslaved workers who created and sang them.

In time, the music of the fields blended with other forms of music, such as the **ballad.** Ballads, which tell stories in several verses, were a favorite of white Americans and Europeans, particularly Celts. Rhythmic, African-based dance songs called jump-ups also came into the mix.

All these musical styles came together to create a music that was not linked solely to Africa or Europe. It was a rich, new music unique to America—and closely tied to the black experience in the American South. By the last decades of the 1800s, America's first wholly black folk music was being born all across the South. That music was the blues.

MUSIC WAS AN IMPORTANT PART OF AFRICAN-AMERICAN LIFE IN THE SOUTH. IN THIS 1872 ILLUSTRATION, A FIDDLER PLAYS A SONG TO ENTERTAIN HIS FAMILY.

Freedom

Black cat on my doorstep, black cat on my windowsill,
Black cat on my doorstep, black cat on my windowsill,
If some black cat don't cross me, some other black cat will.
—From "Black Cat Hoot Owl Blues"
by Gertrude "Ma" Rainey (1928)

From 1861 until 1865, a bitter fight raged in the United States. The North wanted to end slavery. The Southern states needed enslaved workers to keep the plantations running. When no compromise could be found, the divided nation entered into the Civil War. At long last, the North was victorious. General Robert E. Lee, who had led the South, surrendered on April 9, 1865. Slavery in the United States had officially come to an end.

Sudden freedom did not immediately lead to a better life for most African-Americans, however. Most still faced extreme poverty, homelessness, and **racism.** Often, their lives were little better than they had been as slaves. With nowhere to go, many continued working on the plantations where they had spent their lives as slaves. Others became **sharecroppers.** Thousands left their old lives, hoping to find something better somewhere else.

For the first time, African-Americans were free to choose where and how to live. It was a dramatic and welcome change for the former slaves. Finding a new place in everyday life did not come easily, however. Many black men and women experienced deep loneliness. Throughout the South, men roamed from place to place looking for work. As they wandered, they sang of their troubles. They shared what they knew about music, picking up lyrics and melodies from one another. They used what they heard to make up their own new tunes and passed these new songs along.

THE END OF SLAVERY DID LITTLE TO IMPROVE
THE DAILY LIVES OF MANY ENSLAVED WORKERS.

EARLY BLUES SINGERS OFTEN PERFORMED IN JUKE JOINTS. THIS JUKE JOINT SERVED
AS A MEETING PLACE FOR SEASONAL WORKERS IN FLORIDA IN 1941.

Much of this musical exchange took place in small, cabinlike bars called juke joints. Scattered across plantations and hidden in the back woods, juke joints provided cheap drinks, music, and, often, dancing. The juke joint was a place where a good blues singer had the chance to make a few dollars. The first juke joint singers rarely were women. The blues was a rough, raw kind of music that many believed was improper for women to sing.

The blues was a creative expression of the challenges and rewards of black life in America. Blues singers sang of backbreaking work and celebrations, heartache and new love, fear and courage, loss and hope. They sang in power-packed voices about the grief—and joys— they had seen.

After the Civil War, traveling shows became a popular form of entertainment. In some traveling acts called medicine shows, men went from town to town selling medicines. Singers and musicians were frequently hired to draw a crowd and boost sales. It made no difference if they were men or women. As long as people hung around to listen, the singer had a job.

Few bluesmen could make enough money simply from singing. Many were forced to join work crews building railroads or canals. Some ended up in prison, working on chain gangs.

The call-and-response song was a familiar part of life for these men. A strong lead would call out a line of song. The rest of the gang or crew would act as a choir, repeating the line. Then the leader would follow up with a new line, rhyming it with the first. This pattern of two repeated lines followed by a third rhyming line is still a basic characteristic of the blues.

The songs were usually made up on the spot. The topic of the song might be the cruelty of the gang boss, trouble with the law, or feelings for a sweetheart. Also, the songs most often followed the rhythm of the work.

The music's rhythm reflected the pounding of hammers or the lifting and passing of heavy objects from one man to the next. In this way, the gang worked smoothly together, like a well-tuned machine.

WORK CREWS, SUCH AS THESE TEXAS LABORERS IN 1934, WORKED AND SANG TOGETHER.

During times of leisure, singers performed with musical instruments. An early bluesman plays a banjo on his front porch in 1902.

Because there was no place for musical instruments at work, these early blues tunes relied solely on the human voice. At the end of the day, however, workers laid down the tools of the job and picked up guitars and banjos. They brought out their harmonicas and their **bone clappers.** This music carried the rhythms of song and dance that had developed during the days of slavery. Always, the lyrics described the difficulties as well as the pleasures of everyday life.

Skill in playing this music had nothing to do with formal musical education and everything to do with listening. Men and women developed their own blues sounds by copying the styles and techniques of those before them. The music changed and grew through imitation and invention.

Much invention took place in a part of the South called the Mississippi Delta. At the turn of the twentieth century, the Delta was a region of poverty, heat, and racial **prejudice.** It was also home to many legendary early bluesmen. If any single place can be considered the birthplace of the blues, it is the Delta.

AFRICAN-AMERICAN WORKERS FISH NEAR A MISSISSIPPI DELTA COTTON PLANTATION IN 1939. POVERTY WAS A WAY OF LIFE FOR MANY PEOPLE IN THIS PART OF THE UNITED STATES.

Mississippi Delta Blues

The first time I met the blues, mama, they came walking through the wood.
The first time I met the blues, baby, they came walking through the wood.
They stopped at my house first, mama, and done me all the harm they could.
—FROM "THE FIRST TIME I MET YOU"
BY LITTLE BROTHER MONTGOMERY (1936)

In the late 1800s, the South was busy rebuilding itself after the destruction of the Civil War. Much of this reconstruction was centered in the Mississippi Delta region.

The Delta is a long, narrow area that stretches roughly from Vicksburg, Mississippi, to Memphis, Tennessee. It lies between the Mississippi River on the west and the Yazoo River on the east. Some of the worst prison farms and work camps were located here. Where there were work camps, there were blues singers.

BLUES MUSIC THRIVED AT PRISON FARMS AND WORK CAMPS IN THE MISSISSIPPI DELTA REGION.

Hoping for higher-paying work, thousands of blacks moved to the Delta. By the 1890s, the black population was more heavily concentrated in this region than anywhere else in the South. Blacks there outnumbered whites three to one. Also by this time, the blues had spread throughout most of the rural South. But it was in the Delta region that the music was developing most rapidly.

The people moving to the Delta sought jobs in the region's booming construction camps and on land-clearing crews. Others were forcibly brought to these sites. Most were treated harshly and died on the job.

Others were cast aside when they were no longer useful workers.

In this setting of human suffering, music was a rich source of expression and comfort. Men sang of their working woes. They also sang of the things that brought them some small sense of power or gladness.

Like all blues, the Delta style was based on the call-and-response tradition. But it took a slightly different form. The singer, usually playing a guitar, would sing a line of his song. For the second, repeated line of music, he would play his guitar without singing.

THE BLUES HAVE ALWAYS BEEN A PERSONAL EXPRESSION OF EMOTION. THIS BLUESMAN FROM THE 1930s SINGS A BALLAD.

Another feature of the Delta blues was the slide guitar. The slide was an object that the guitarist held against the guitar strings as he played. The most common slide was either the flat blade of a knife or a broken glass bottleneck slipped onto a finger. (Today's manufactured metal slides are still called bottlenecks.) The sound came from pressing the slide firmly up and down the strings. At the same time, the guitarist would pluck separate notes with his other hand.

The Delta bluesmen played together, sharing what they learned and spreading their new music. A voice, the slide guitar, and often a harmonica— together with the second-line guitar response—created an instantly recognizable sound. Now, anyone who plays the blues in this style is said to be playing the Delta blues.

Moving Out, Moving Up

I hate to see de ev'nin' sun go down,
Hate to see de ev'nin' sun go down,
'Cause my baby, he done left this town.
—From "St. Louis Blues"
by W. C. Handy (1914)

As the 1800s gave way to the 1900s, the music being called the blues was moving out of rural areas and into towns and cities throughout the South. By 1910, the expression "the blues" was commonly used in the United States to describe this kind of music.

People were talking about the blues. It was sometimes even mentioned in writing. But the music itself was still only something to listen to. Most people who sang and played the blues could not read music. They could not read at all. With few exceptions, no one had written down the words or the music to these field songs. Not a single blues singer had ever been recorded.

LITTLE IS KNOWN ABOUT THE EARLIEST BLUES MUSICIANS, SUCH AS BLIND LEMON JEFFERSON, SHOWN HERE IN THE 1920s.

BLUES COMPOSER, PUBLISHER, AND TEACHER
W. C. HANDY HOLDS A TRUMPET IN ABOUT
1915. HANDY BEGAN HIS MUSIC CAREER
PLAYING IN A TRAVELING SHOW.

Finally, in about 1912, sheet music for a few blues tunes began to appear. Most of this printed music came from New Orleans, Louisiana, and St. Louis, Missouri. Although historians disagree about who wrote down the first blues song, they agree that a composer named William Christopher "W. C." Handy was the first to bring the blues to a wider audience. In 1903, while waiting for a train in Tutwiler, Mississippi, Handy first heard the blues, played by a man on a slide guitar. Handy called it "the weirdest music" he had ever heard and copied it down.

In 1909, Handy composed a blues tune himself. He called this song "Memphis Blues." The tune, finally published in 1912, helped the blues gain much early attention.

Two years later, Handy published his greatest blues tune, "St. Louis Blues." That skillful, soulful song seemed to launch a blues craze that hit the North as well as the South.

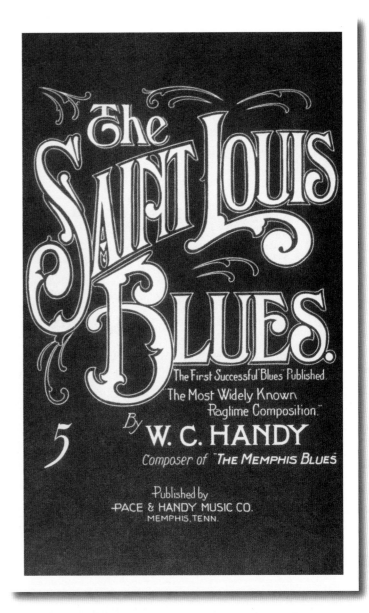

"ST. LOUIS BLUES" BY W. C. HANDY WAS FIRST PUBLISHED IN 1914.

Since its publication in 1914, "St. Louis Blues" has been recorded by numerous artists. Hollywood films have featured the song. It is a standard tune of today's **jazz** and blues musicians.

"St. Louis Blues" was published the year World War I began. In 1917, the United States joined the war, and the blues spread to Europe with the U.S. troops—and the 369th Infantry Regiment band.

JAZZ GREAT LOUIS ARMSTRONG GETS READY TO PLAY THE FAMOUS "ST. LOUIS BLUES" IN 1950.

THE HELLFIGHTERS ARRIVE IN NEW YORK CITY AFTER WORLD WAR I.
IN ADDITION TO SERVING IN COMBAT, THEY PERFORMED BLUES AND JAZZ
MUSIC OVERSEAS.

Known as the Hellfighters, the 369th Infantry Regiment band was acclaimed for its courage in combat. The African-American Hellfighters, led by James Reese Europe, were celebrated off the battlefield as well. The band's spirited performances of **ragtime** numbers, jazz hits, and Handy originals caused a huge sensation with the troops and the general public. By the time they returned to U.S. soil, the Hellfighters were legendary at home and abroad.

The blues craze demanded records. In addition to listening to bluesmen, people wanted to hear the powerful, moving voices of women singers. The first blues tune ever recorded, "Crazy Blues," was cut in 1920 by a woman named Mamie Smith. Recordings by many great blues singers—male and female—followed.

By the 1920s, blues music had spread far from the original humble juke joints. It was gaining an audience in large parts of the North. Those who could express the most powerfully moving feelings were considered the best singers. If the singer didn't genuinely feel it, the opinion went, it wasn't worth listening to.

There was plenty of blues music worth listening to in the 1920s and 1930s. This period is sometimes called the golden age of the blues.

During this time, much of the best blues music was coming from female singers. These women sang of love and pain and death as powerfully as the men did. As the music of the blues became more familiar, it became more popular. These distinct female voices added a new richness and depth to the blues. They took the music to even greater heights.

MAMIE SMITH, SHOWN HERE IN 1920 WITH THE JAZZ HOUNDS IN NEW YORK CITY, SOLD MORE THAN ONE MILLION COPIES OF HER RECORDING OF "CRAZY BLUES."

The Blues Makes a Name

Blind Boy had a million friends, North, East, South and West,
Blind Boy had a million friends, North, East, South and West,
Yes, you know it's hard to tell which place he was loved the best.
—From "The Death of Blind Boy Fuller"
by Brownie McGhee (1941)

The names of Gertrude "Ma" Rainey, Bessie Smith (no relation to Mamie), and Billie Holiday rank at the top of the list of greatest female blues singers. Bessie Smith was born in Chattanooga, Tennessee, in 1894. She began singing in traveling shows of the South when she was about 13 years old. There, she briefly worked with Rainey.

After working in traveling shows for eight years, Bessie Smith managed to put together her own show. In 1923, her first record, "Downhearted Blues," was released. It sold an incredible 780,000 copies. During her lifetime, Smith's fame as a blues singer was greater than any other artist, man or woman. Even today, she is known as the Empress of the Blues.

GERTRUDE RAINEY WAS KNOWN AS THE MOTHER OF THE BLUES.

BESSIE SMITH, SHOWN HERE IN 1923, WAS A FAVORITE OF THE JAZZ PUBLIC.

Billie Holiday came of age in the 1930s. She wanted to sing like Bessie Smith, but Holiday did not have Smith's large, powerful voice. Instead, listeners were deeply affected by Holiday's sorrowful voice. Her life was short and sad. She died in 1959 at the age of 44. The impact of Billie Holiday's music is felt even today.

Many other extremely gifted female blues singers stood in the limelight in the 1920s and 1930s. Usually, they were backed by a band of male musicians. Unlike the women, the male blues singers usually played a guitar or some other instrument. Not surprisingly, many of these musicians came from the Mississippi Delta.

The long list of famous early Delta bluesmen includes Son House, Charlie Patton, Big Bill Broonzy, and Robert Johnson. Later came Delta stars such as Muddy Waters, Howlin' Wolf, Elmore James, Bo Diddley, and B. B. King.

Robert Johnson was especially important in developing a style that others later copied. Following the Delta tradition, Johnson played with a bottleneck or metal slide. People claimed to be haunted by his music. They said his high-pitched voice was the sound of sorrow itself. Sometimes it was difficult to tell when Johnson's voice ended and his guitar playing began. Robert Johnson was only 27 when he died in 1938, but modern-day blues players continue to look up to him.

Many bluesmen who left Mississippi moved north to big cities of the Midwest such as Chicago, Illinois, and Detroit, Michigan. McKinley Morganfield was one of these bluesmen. He was nicknamed Muddy Waters at an early age. He grew up on a Mississippi plantation and quit school at the age of 10 to work in the cotton fields. His first instrument was the harmonica. After hearing the music of Johnson and Son House, Waters began playing guitar, too. In 1943, at the age of 28, he landed in Chicago.

MUDDY WATERS PLAYS THE SLIDE GUITAR. HIS MUSIC INFLUENCED POPULAR MUSICIANS SUCH AS CHUCK BERRY, ERIC CLAPTON, AND MICK JAGGER.

Like many other less famous Delta bluesmen before him, Muddy Waters made Chicago his home. Playing together, the musicians there found new ways to express the blues. Their sound grew and changed. Over time, this new style of sound came to be called the Chicago blues. Although Chicago wasn't the birthplace of the blues, it is often called the home of the blues.

In the late 1940s, some artists began experimenting with music that came to be called **rhythm and blues,** or R&B. This music featured electric instruments and a strong beat. R&B artists included singers Ruth Brown and Louis Jordan, trumpeter and bandleader Louis Prima, and keyboard giant Professor Longhair.

One of the most famous blues musicians of all time is B. B. King. He had his first hit record, "Three O'Clock Blues," in 1952. He was only 27. Born in Mississippi, King rarely left the South in his younger years. Now B. B. King and his gut-wrenching blues sound—played on his guitar named Lucille—are known and loved around the world.

The blues is one of America's earliest original folk music styles. It is music that has felt the influence of both African and European traditions. In turn, it has been an important source for other kinds of western music.

Blues musicians were perhaps the first to invent their music as they went along. The invention began as a single line of melody and lyrics made up on the spot in the fields. Later, musicians took simple guitar **riffs** and turned them into long, inventive melodies. This kind of **improvisation** is an important part of playing the blues even today.

WHEN HE WAS 23, B. B. KING, SHOWN HERE IN 1979, PLAYED ON A MEMPHIS, TENNESSEE, RADIO STATION AS THE BEALE STREET BLUES BOY. IT WAS LATER SHORTENED TO "B. B."

Improvisation may have started with the blues, but it also came to be part of jazz music. Jazz borrowed much from the blues as it began to develop in the early 1900s. Many of the earliest blues melodies became standard jazz pieces. These blues tunes were given a jazz flavor and passed down.

The blues has also had a huge influence on rock music. White rock bands of the 1960s and 1970s were deeply affected by Muddy Waters and B. B. King, among other blues musicians. The Rolling Stones, Canned Heat, Cream (with Eric Clapton), The Who, and dozens of others caught the intensity of the blues. They used the different blues techniques to invent their own blues-based rock styles.

THE ROLLING STONES, SHOWN HERE IN 1964 IN LONDON, ENGLAND, TOOK THEIR NAME FROM A SONG BY BLUES GREAT MUDDY WATERS.

Starting in the 1960s, the blues became increasingly popular with white audiences. College students were, and continue to be, especially big fans. At the same time, most African-Americans were losing interest in the music. They were moving on to the more romantic and personal soul music sound.

Throughout the years, the blues has endured. In fact, much of today's music—including country, folk, classical, and hip-hop—shows the influence of the blues tradition. Of course, it continues to be a vital music style in its own right, performed by artists such as Buddy Guy, Etta James, Taj Mahal, Corey Harris, Bonnie Raitt, Robert Cray, John Lee Hooker, and of course, B. B. King. The blues keeps growing and changing just as it always has.

BLUES LEGEND JOHN LEE HOOKER PERFORMS IN SAN JOSE, CALIFORNIA, IN 1998. HE DIED IN 2001.

The powerful effects of the blues dig deep into the feelings of its fans. The blues recalls the loss, humiliation, and cruelty suffered by the enslaved workers long ago. It is music that calls on its listeners to feel and to be moved by the emotions of the great blues artists. Not just a stream of woeful tales, it also calls on joy. It is a music that is raw, wild, spirited, and, much of the time, full of celebration.

The birth of the blues as an art form tells the story of terrible human suffering. But that birthing also contains the story of courage and triumph. It is a record of songs of hopelessness. These songs have always served to keep hope alive, too. Listening to the blues is a way of remembering these things—and that may be the music's most important gift.

ETTA JAMES IS ONE OF MANY GIFTED PERFORMERS OF THE UNIQUELY AMERICAN MUSIC CALLED THE BLUES.

Timeline

1820s–mid-1800s	Slaves begin to develop call-and-response songs influenced by Western and African culture, such as the field holler and the spiritual.
1865	Northern states win the Civil War. The enslaved people are given their freedom.
1870	As they move through the South, traveling shows hire African-Americans to sing and dance.
1890s	African-Americans travel through the South seeking jobs and spreading their music to others. As they move along the Mississippi River, their music begins to move north.
1903	While waiting for a train in Tutwiler, Mississippi, American composer W. C. Handy first hears a man playing slide guitar. He calls it "the weirdest music" he ever heard and copies it down.
1905	Gertrude "Ma" Rainey hears an early blues singer and puts this music into her own show. Others follow her lead.
1912	W. C. Handy publishes his first blues song, "Memphis Blues."
1920	Mamie Smith records the first blues record, "Crazy Blues."
1920s	The Library of Congress hires John and Alan Lomax to make field recordings of folk and blues music.
1930s	Many Mississippi Delta blues singers move to northern cities, bringing their music with them.
1932	The electric guitar is invented and begins to transform the sound of the blues.
1940s	Blues singers continue to move north and west. Rhythm and blues, or R&B, played with electric guitars begins to take root in the United States.
1941	The blues becomes part of a regular radio show in Arkansas. The show's success encourages other radio stations to hire blues singers. W. C. Handy publishes his autobiography, *Father of the Blue*.
1950s	The "Chicago blues" style is popularized by stars such as Muddy Waters, Howlin' Wolf, T-Bone Walker, and B. B. King.
1960s	The blues enjoys a widespread revival of public interest. Many white rock musicians incorporate the blues into their own music.
1980	Blues artists win the first W. C. Handy Awards to honor the year's outstanding performances.
1982	The Grammy Award for Best Traditional Blues Recording is given for the first time.
1988	The Rhythm and Blues Foundation is founded for the historical and cultural preservation of R&B.
1996	B. B. King publishes his autobiography, *Blues All around Me*.
2003	The U.S. Congress declares 2003 the Year of the Blues.

Glossary

ballad (BAL-uhd)
A ballad is a popular song with romantic themes. The ballad was a favorite of white Americans and Europeans.

blues (BLOOZ)
The blues is a sad kind of music first created by African-Americans. Many historians think that field songs of the South were probably where the music known as the blues began.

bone clappers (BOHN KLAP-urz)
Bone clappers are carved bone, wood, or ivory musical instruments that open and shut with the hand to make a clapping sound. Early blues musicians played bone clappers as well as guitars, banjos, and harmonicas.

improvisation (im-prov-uh-ZAY-shuhn)
Improvisation is the ability to compose or create new music on the spot, often using the basic chords of a specific song as a guide. Improvisation is an important part of playing the blues.

jazz (JAZ)
Jazz is an American music that developed from ragtime and blues music in the early 1900s. It features syncopated or irregular beats and accents, improvisation, and an instrumental style that often imitates the voice.

lyrics (LIHR-ix)
Lyrics are the words of a song. Blues lyrics have always dealt with troubled states of mind.

prejudice (PREJ-uh-diss)
Prejudice is a fixed or unfair opinion about someone based on his or her race or religion. At the turn of the twentieth century, the Mississippi Delta was a region of poverty, heat, and racial prejudice.

racism (RAY-sih-zim)
Racism is a negative feeling or opinion about people because of their race. Freed slaves often still faced poverty, homelessness, and racism.

ragtime (RAG-time)
Ragtime is an early style of jazz with a strong, regular beat. During World War I, the all-black 369th Infantry division, known as the Hellfighters, performed ragtime numbers, jazz hits, and Handy originals for the troops and general public overseas.

rhythm and blues (RITH-uhm and BLOOZ)
Rhythm and blues, or R&B, is an American popular music influenced by the blues. In the late 1940s, some artists began experimenting with music that came to be called rhythm and blues.

riffs (RYFFS)
Riffs are melodic phrases that draw on a tune's theme. Blues musicians often take simple guitar riffs and turn them into long, inventive melodies.

sharecroppers (SHAIR-krop-purz)
Sharecroppers are workers who farm the land for the owner in return for part of the crops. After the end of the Civil War, freed slaves often worked as sharecroppers.

Index

Further Information

Books

Asirvatham, Sandy. *The History of the Blues.* Broomall, Penn.: Chelsea House Publishing, 2003.

Elmer, Howard. *Blues: Its Birth and Growth.* New York: Rosen Publishing Group, 1999.

Lester, Julius, and Lisa Cohen (illustrator). *The Blues Singers: Ten Who Rocked the World.* New York: Jump at the Sun/Hyperion Books for Children, 2001.

Summer, L. S. *W. C. Handy: Founder of the Blues.* Chanhassen, Minn.: The Child's World, 2002.

Web Sites

Visit our homepage for lots of links about the blues:

http://www.childsworld.com/links.html

Note to Parents, Teachers, and Librarians:
We routinely verify our Web links to make sure they're safe, active sites—so encourage your readers to check them out!

About the Author

In the past decade, Pamela Dell has published 22 children's books, both fiction and nonfiction, and has also created award-winning educational and entertainment software for children. She divides her time between Santa Monica, California, and Chicago, Illinois.